MICHAL STAWICKI

POWER UP

YOUR

SELF-

TALK

6 SIMPLE HABITS TO STOP BEATING YOURSELF UP AND RECLAIM YOUR LIFE

TABLE OF CONTENTS

CHAPTER 1

THE POWERFUL PROBLEM

Hey, you worthless *piece of shit! Yes, I'm talking to you!*

Are you mad at me?

What kind of self-help book is this, if an author starts it that way?

Maybe you are outraged. How dare I say such heinous things about you? How dare I judge you so harshly and obscenely?

> *The way you talk to yourself is worse, certainly,*
> *than the way anyone else talks to you.*
> – Seth Godin

I just wanted to make a point. There is a pretty high probability that you've said much worse things to yourself. And you didn't become mad or outraged. Instead, you consented.

I purposefully started the book with this outrageous insult. If you cannot stand invective from me, how can you stand self-inflicted verbal abuse? I wanted to evoke anger. I wanted you to stop hiding the problem you have. I wanted you to acknowledge that you insult yourself like this and much worse, and you do it without purpose or reason. You go overboard with it and it **destroys** your life like **nothing else**.

And I want you to do something about it. Read this book. Learn how to change your self-talk for good. Stop being your worst critic, tormentor, judge, and hangman. Turn your life around.

I'll keep the language in this book civil and will refrain from referring to excrement from now on. The only ugly expressions you will find in it will be examples of negative self-talk.

Well, if you were mad because I insulted you and you've never said any crap to yourself, I'm sorry, and this book is clearly not for you. You are above negative self-talk and already live happily ever after. I'm so glad for you! People like you are like sunshine for this world. Thank you for being the best version of yourself.

However, very few people are like that. In fact, virtually everyone I've ever met in real life (not in the magical bubble of social media) was struggling with their self-talk and this struggle was always at the source of their life struggles. We judge ourselves harshly. We belittle ourselves. We are full of self-doubts and self-loathing.

When I wrote my book about overcoming shyness, *From Shy to Hi*, I shared negative thoughts that crossed my mind when I was about to approach a stranger and start a conversation. It was a real slop bucket. I was blown away when every beta reader I shared the advanced reading copy with said: "Yeah, me too. I tell myself such atrocious stuff all too often."

That was the first time I'd ever gotten confirmation that I was not a lonely madman. We all share this affliction. I started to see this theme again and again. Self-talk was affecting everything I was teaching about.

For example, if you want to change your personal philosophy (the topic of my book *Trickle Down Mindset*), you must pay attention to your self-talk, or it may undermine everything you want to accomplish. You may read zillions of personal development books and listen to gurus around the clock, but it's to no avail if your self-talk torpedoes everything you consume.

"Well, this guy had it easy; I, on the other hand..."

"Bollocks! I don't have his money/friends/wits, so it's impossible for me."

"Yes, I wish I was like him, but I'm not. I'm a worthless piece of sh..."

If you want to develop persistence and follow one course of action for the long haul (the topic of *The Art of Persistence*), your first obstacle is your self-talk. Whatever you say to yourself about persistence, or about the discipline you resolved to follow, will affect your performance. That's the reason only 9% of folks succeed with their New Year's resolutions. The rest tell themselves ugly things, especially after the first failure to keep their commitment. And they quit.

Crappy self-talk is also the main reason that only 42% of Americans even bother making a New Year's resolution. Instead of attempting to change their lives, they simply say to themselves: "I'm no good. I'll fail anyway, so why bother?"

Voices in your head are robbing you of your money when you spend it on useless trinkets like a fifteenth fridge magnet to feel the boost of shopping-induced dopamine. They rob you of your health when you reach out for junk food or roll over and go back to bed instead of going out for a morning jog.

What you say to yourself determines if you will do your job well. In fact, your self-talk often determines if you do any work at all. And it's your negative self-talk that makes you lash out at your spouse or your children, not what they've done or said to you.

No one can make you feel inferior without your consent.
– Eleanor Roosevelt

IT WON'T BE EASY

Make no mistake, changing your self-talk is not an easy feat. The more negative it is and the longer you've lived with it, the harder it will be. That's not a threat, it's a statement of fact. You've been conditioned for years to say the worst possible things to yourself. It is likely you haven't taken even a first step towards reaching your full potential in decades.

However, no matter how hard it is going to be, you have no other choice. Well, not a real choice. You may choose to ignore this book and this advice or quit after a few first feeble attempts. That means you choose your current reality and accept that it can only worsen. Negative self-talk will rub your face in the mud and keep you there forever.

If you give up, nothing can change. A knight on a white stallion won't magically appear to save you from health, financial, career, or relationship problems caused by harmful self-talk. You'll be stuck with those ugly voices in your head for good. This is not an option to consider.

There is no labor from which most people shrink as they do from that of sustained and consecutive thought. It is the hardest work in the world.
– Wallace D. Wattles

Affecting your self-talk involves thinking at the highest levels. It's not a mindless exercise like jogging. What is more, it involves sustained and focused thinking. There is no harder job in the known universe.

Prepare for that in advance. Embrace the struggle. It is a necessary part of the process. Your job is to overcome the resistance of years of faulty thinking, maybe even long decades. Put everything you have into it. Commit to change or die trying. Because listening to the savage voice in your head is worse than death. It's like a hell on earth.

BUT IT WILL BE SIMPLE

The things I'll teach you are simple. Some of them are incredibly simple. But that doesn't make them easy.

If you keep it simple, it will get easier.

In the end, no matter how hard this job of turning around your self-talk seems to be, it's doable. You are not the first person in the history of humanity who will stop telling yourself derogatory things and will start living up to your potential.

There were countless others before you who did exactly the same thing. I suspect that 99% of great people in history somehow overcame their self-talk and mastered their thinking to serve them, not chain them.

If one man did that before, you can hope to do it too.

If hundreds and thousands have done that, you know it's a teachable skill. I will teach you this skill.

CHAPTER 2

THE POWER OF MY STORY

I wrote this book because I couldn't find any book like it. I got sick of writing in every review of a self-help book I read:

"The author has an expert's bias. He naively thinks that his readers are capable of actually steering their thought processes."

I mean, yes, we all can think, we are human beings. But the level of thinking that self-help authors require from their readers is a rare art.

People rarely consciously examine themselves. It's even rarer to stop yourself in your tracks and ask yourself a question that discredits what you are currently doing. We are used to functioning on autopilot. Guess who the real pilot is behind the steering wheel of your life?

Your subconscious.

And it reveals itself through your self-talk. Most of the time, the autopilot of your life is a drunken felon. Or at least you can suspect that by its vocabulary.

Since no one else noticed or properly tackled this problem, I decided to write a book about it. Or rather, not a book *about* the problem, but a detailed step-by-step guide on how to *solve* this problem, one reader at the time.

I wrote the words above in April 2018. Six years prior, I was a totally average person, with totally crappy self-talk. "I'm a failure" or "It won't work" were the sentences I used most in my internal communication. I'll spare you the more obscene terms I had been using in my self-talk. You'd find a lot of f-bombs and excrement-related sayings. I used them habitually, not even truly thinking about what I was saying.

"Totally average" meant that I had a day job and a family, and I lived just to get by. Monday-morning syndrome, long commute to work, weekend syndrome, and an absolute lack of purpose were inherent parts of my life.

I lived a life of quiet desperation. I was constantly frustrated. I knew I should be able to achieve more, but I didn't really believe I could change anything. I felt stuck.

Whenever I even played with the thought of doing something more with my life, my self-talk stopped me right in my tracks. I told myself I was a failure and failures don't succeed, so what was the sense in even trying? And most of the time, I abandoned any idea of improving my life just by thinking ugly thoughts about myself and my abilities.

The few times I tried something, I quickly gave up because my subconscious was very quick to point out my flaws and failures. And they were real flaws and failures because I was at the lowest of my abilities. You always are at your lowest at the beginning of anything. It's only natural to fail when you start something unfamiliar. But my crappy self-talk was always there like a guard of my inner prison, ready to point out my every stumble and bring me back to the status quo.

I was terrified to make any changes in my life. In fact, I was convinced I didn't *want* any change in my life, even though I felt aimless. And my self-talk kept me in check, providing useful invectives whenever the pain of the existential void grew too much to bear, and I was timidly trying to change that.

But I've changed. A big part of my life transformation was triggered by the change in my self-talk. For the first year or so, I didn't even consciously try to affect my self-talk. I tried to achieve something more with my life. I used many different methods and some of them had quite a direct influence on what I was saying to myself daily.

About a year ago I started reviewing self-help books regularly. I quickly noticed that authors were all blind to the fact that normal people cannot steer their internal dialog proficiently. Thus, many readers got little to nothing out of the information in their books.

I'm not very bright. Only after noticing the same problem for the fifth or tenth time did I decide to do something about it—write a book that teaches people how to change their self-talk for good.

I reverse-engineered all the techniques I had used that affected my self-talk. I created a big part of this arsenal while I was over-coming my shyness. If you are shy, you know what I'm talking about. Whenever I tried to approach a stranger and start a conversation, a constant trickle of murmurs whispered to me about my self-worth, attractiveness (even though I had no romantic relationship in mind *AT ALL*), and general sanity very negatively.

This book consists solely of methods that I used and found helpful. I arranged them by their level of difficulty, starting with the easiest one. They can all be practiced on a daily basis and this is how I used them. Convert a self-help method into a habit and the benefits will compound and last for a lifetime.

PROGRESS NOT PERFECTION

My self-talk is still self-defeating all too often. That's why I'll be your best teacher. Not only do I know where you are, I can feel it in my gut. That is also why gurus cannot help you. Their memories of nasty self-talk have faded. Their knowledge is more intellectual than from actual experience. Anthony Robbins is not your go-to person right now because he is now full of positive thoughts from his feet up to his ears. He thinks that he is an awesome dude. Why shouldn't he? He is.

You and I are only on the road to awesomeness, and if your self-talk is still full of self-directed f-bombs, I am a bit further ahead.

Negative self-talk still oozes from my mind, *but*—and it is a *big* but—it no longer disarms me. I can still take action despite my self-talk. I can deflect, ignore, or overcome my internal negativity. I'm no longer a victim; I'm a fighter.

Only if you fight can you win. And if you don't give up, no one can beat you. Keep going or die trying.

Come on! Let's make a fighter of you!

CHAPTER 3

THE POWER OF JOY

I think the biggest weakness of all the self-help books I read is that they try to force you, a reader, to do something you are not capable of yet. The famous "ask yourself" thing. Don't get me wrong; we are capable of asking ourselves introspective questions. The problem is, we are not used to it. I bet not even 10% of readers stop reading at such a command and do the prescribed exercise in the first place. And almost no one does such self-reflection habitually.

Thus, I will start with something ridiculously easy that you are capable of right here, right now, and can repeat many times a day. Repetition is the key to developing a habit. I strongly believe that if you don't embrace a new behavior in a habitual manner, you cannot change yourself.

Method #1 is in the realm of abilities of every common mortal. Here it goes: *smile.*

Are you capable of that ultra-complicated self-help activity? *wink* Of course, you are!

If you doubt me, force a smile on your face right now! If you don't doubt me, smile as well. Make the corners of your mouth curl up a bit. Make it wider. Alright! You've just smiled!

I've gone through periods of depression in my life, and I know sometimes it's really hard to smile. I get it! But you need to start somewhere, and smiling is the easiest thing to do. Well, winking might be easier, but a wink won't help you with your self-talk; a smile will.

You must smile even if you don't feel like it. That's the whole point of the exercise. If you have to force your smile—do it! A forced smile is infinitely better than no smile at all. The thing is, it works whether you force it or not. Like with everything else, the only time it doesn't work is when you don't do it at all.

Why does the forced smile work? Because we are creatures of habit. Flex your facial muscles in a way that forms a smile on your face, and your brain gets the same physiological signals it has been getting your whole life when you've smiled. The habit loop is triggered. Your brain responds by releasing endorphins. You are feeling better. It works.

This habit loop of releasing happiness-inducing hormones has been forming your whole life. It's part of your body's chemistry already. You would need an awesome charge of mindfulness and years of training to revert this mechanism. Every time you smiled in the past, a chemical "happy soup" was released into your bloodstream. It's automatic. Smile equals happiness.

Of course, a genuine smile works even better. But you know the saying: "Better is the enemy of good." Don't chase genuineness if you cannot generate it. It's much easier to flex your face in a contortion imitating a smile than to forge a genuine positive emotion that will make you smile.

If you can think of something nice—recall a positive event or a warm interaction with your loved ones—go for it. If you need a piece of chocolate to bring a smile to your face, eat one. Just remembering the consumption of a delicious piece of chocolate can probably recall this feeling as well as actually eating a piece of it.

When your smile is genuine, the charge of positivity is bigger. It is as simple as that. However, don't chase "bigger" at the cost of "anything."

> *Objects in motion tend to stay in motion.*
> *Objects at rest tend to stay at rest.*
> – Newton's First Law of motion

If you wait in vain for a good mood to smile, the number of your smiles is zero. Zero multiplied by infinity is still a zero. Start where you are and do something.

If necessary, force your smile.

LEVERAGE THE POWER OF HABIT

You should smile as often as possible (and then some). I've never heard of overdosing on smiles. I encourage you to challenge yourself. Count your smiles in the first day and try to double the number the next day. Or think of the highest possible number of smiles you can summon on your face and try to hit or exceed this number.

Most of the times you will underestimate your smiling potential.

I read a story of a high achiever who hired a former marine to help him work on his fitness. The marine made him do an insane number of pull-ups on the first day only to illustrate to the guy that he was capable of much more than he thought he was. And remember, his muscles were screaming in pain, his body was telling him it was impossible. When you smile, the only thing that eventually may scream is your mind. A creation of your exuberant imagination.

The best way to go about it is to habitualize your smiling. Why is it the best way? Your self-talk is habitual to the core. If you want to stand a chance against it, you need to use a similar weapon.

For me, the trigger for this habit is seeing another person in front of me. I worked hard on this when I was overcoming my shyness.

It was the first tool I used. I was unable to start a conversation with a stranger, but smiling at them was easier for me and not dependent on their reactions or cooperation. Now it's purely automatic. Whenever I see another person approaching, I smile. Period.

As much I appreciate this habit as a socializing tool, for your purposes it's not necessary to smile at people. Your sole purpose is to smile more, period. Pick your own trigger to create your own smiling habit, the one that will stay with you for life. You can smile to yourself in a bathroom mirror when doing your daily ablutions. You can smile at your pet whenever you see it.

The important point is that you hook your smiling habit to an already-existing activity. That is the easiest way to develop a new habit. Don't discuss it with yourself, don't ponder, just do it. You want to smile when you start brushing your teeth? Do it! Ignore your feelings (*"That feels stupid."*) or discouraging thoughts (*"Smiling? No way it's gonna help you, sucker!"*). Just do it. The habit is created by doing, not by thinking about it.

FOR THE SAKE OF MOOD

Remember our experiment with forcing the smile? The biggest benefit of this method is not direct alteration of your self-talk; it's an immediate improvement of your mood. Negative self-talk keeps you down. It's so much easier to control a person who is feeling low. With your smiles, you don't fight off the self-talk itself, but its repercussions.

Each smile instantly makes you feel better for a moment. And one moment is all you need. It's like catching a swig of fresh air after coming out of a confined space. One smile will not make much of a difference, but you are getting into a habit of smiling, right? You will get more breaks from the down feelings your horrendous self-talk causes. And it will start a ripple effect.

You see, humans are very complicated beings. Everything in your life is interconnected. Your physical shape, your thoughts, your memories, and your emotions mingle together each second and create you as you are. If you input a pinch of positivity into this mix, it will change you. Sure, the change may be miniscule, especially when we talk about the effect of a single smile. But it happens nonetheless.

It works. It's like with smiling through tears. When you do this you are no longer 100% sad, are you?

A smile is like a single tiny candle lighting up the darkness. Even this tiny light disperses the darkness. Even one smile will inject some positivity into your internal life. It's like a pinch of salt that changes the taste of the whole meal. It's not much, but it changes everything.

Once you disperse the darkness a little, once the mud of your negative self-talk loses its suffocating grip on your mind for a moment, once you regain a bit of your mental strength, you can face your self-talk more directly. At the beginning, you just need some breathing space.

And it's important to use natural means to that goal. You can feel better by intoxicating yourself with alcohol or drugs. You can do that by belittling other people. You can even feel better by playing a victim and coercing some compassion from your friends or relatives. But all those "methods" only add to the arsenal of your bullying self-talk. They provide even more ammunition to bring you further down.

Smiling is a healthy, simple, and easy way to feel better and regain some mental strength.

ACTION PLAN

1. **Smile right now!**

   If necessary, force a smile.

2. **Design a smiling habit.**

   Reflect how can you smile more and smile habitually. Every morning in front of a bathroom mirror? Every time you cross a doorstep? Every time you stand up from a chair?

3. **Implement your plan today.**

   Smile at least three times before the day ends within the framework of your plan.

4. **Modify your plan.**

   If you are well-tuned to yourself, there is a good chance your initial plan will work. As long as you are true to yourself, you come up with ideas that are authentic, thus there is no internal resistance against them.

   But if your initial plan doesn't work for you, it's not a reason to quit.

   When it is obvious that the goals cannot be reached,
   don't adjust the goals, adjust the action steps.
   – Confucius

   Think of another way. Implement it. Track it. Rinse and repeat until you are successful.

CHAPTER 4

THE POWER OF FOCUS

The second method for dealing with your self-talk—meditation—is almost as easy as smiling. On the face of it, it's not so. Meditation seems like a challenge for many people for various reasons. However, the data proves that it is almost as easy as flossing your teeth. Coach.me has a base of a few million users. They went through their data and found out that developing a meditation habit was only marginally harder than developing a flossing habit.

How so? In the end, meditation is very natural. Close your eyes. Take a deep breath. Exhale. Those are all basic human activities. You breathe all the time. Moving your eyelids is automatic. You do it all the time to keep your eyes wet enough.

Did you close your eyes a moment ago, inhale and exhale air? So, you are good to go. You are already a meditator.

> *You should sit in meditation for twenty minutes every day*
> *– unless you're too busy. Then you should sit for an hour.*
> – Zen proverb

Meditators who practice meditation for longer than fifteen minutes a day swear by it. Clint Eastwood has been meditating for forty years, and he is in good company with George Lucas, Oprah Winfrey, and many other bigshots. So there must be more than a grain of truth in this saying.

But... (By the way, a tidbit: anything said before "but" doesn't count in your mind.)

But you can't meditate for thirty minutes if you haven't ever meditated before. Well, technically, it's possible, but it's extremely unlikely that you'll be successful. You need to learn the ropes first.

I feel that a two-minute meditation session at the beginning is more than enough. To build a habit, start small and scale up. Again, you need to build habits to deal with your habitual self-talk. Sitting once for thirty minutes and meditating is not a habit.

Going back to the Coach.me data research, they determined that if you start with a two-minute meditation and keep it going for eleven days, then your chance of developing a lasting habit is 90%.

I encourage you to start even smaller. Instead of one two-minute session, try to have a dozen two-breath sessions. Two deep breaths takes you about ten seconds. You can do this activity anywhere— while waiting for a train or an elevator, while walking to the grocery store at the corner, or while standing in a queue at the store. I've meditated on crowded subway trains, in elevators, or while waiting on a train platform.

Frequency of activity translates to number of repetitions and the number of repetitions is the true determinant of a new habit. So, the more repetitions you can stuff into a short time span, the faster you will obtain a lasting habit.

DON'T TRY; DO

The methods of meditation vary wildly. Contrary to appearances, I'm no raving fan of meditation. I'm not especially interested in it, and I didn't study it very much. Yet, even I know several ways of meditation and have tried a few of them. You can focus on your breath, like I suggested in the beginning of this Chapter. You can perform a body scan, focusing your attention on particular parts of your body. You can passively absorb the background sounds of your environment. You can use a guided meditation or listen to a recording of ocean waves.

You can do any of them. Just don't go down the rabbit hole of discovering and trying every method. Stop learning and start doing as soon as possible.

No matter which method of meditation you consider, they all have one thing in common: they steer your attention to very simple things, like the flow of air through your nostrils or how your back feels against a wall.

And this is where the magic happens. When you try to focus your mind on such simple things for an extended period, your mind rebels. It is used to spawning a constant string of thoughts. It loves to think about complex things, especially social interactions. And it does this without you even noticing. Breathing? The feeling of your butt on a pillow? "Give me a break!" screams your mind. "This is not interesting at all."

Whichever way you practice meditation, such random thoughts will come uninvited. And guess what? You will finally notice them.

Random thoughts will bounce in your head, that's a given. Your conscious attention will be focused on something else and suddenly a thought about your to-do items, a flashback to a morning interaction with your spouse, some self-directed comment, or a memory will pop into your head. That's completely normal. While an empty mind is a good thing to aspire to during meditation, it's the end goal, not the process itself. Think of it as being like when you try to keep your balance. You never stand completely still. You flex your core or leg muscles continuously to keep your balance.

Flexing your muscles keeps you balanced. Dealing with uninvited thoughts keeps you in meditation. The basic way to deal with your distracted mind is to move your focus back to square one.

Focus again on the flow of air in your nostrils. Pop! Another thought appears. Focus on the flow of air again. Bounce! You recall an important meeting in your calendar later in the week. Focus on the flow of air. And so on.

This redirecting of your thoughts is the whole point of meditation. True, you get a zillion additional benefits from it. Scientists have correlated meditation practice with numerous health benefits, including lowering blood pressure and an amazingly wide spectrum of other advantages. Your stress level drops, your performance at work increases, and so on.

But they are aftereffects. The real benefit of meditation is that you become aware of your internal chatter.

YOU HAVE A PROBLEM

Do you know what the first step in the Alcoholics Anonymous twelve-step program is? Admit you have a problem. This is what meditation will allow you to do. Your life is automatic beyond your imagination, and your habitual self-talk is the most fossilized of your habits. It's so automatic that you don't even notice that you talk with yourself all the time.

Impulse-response reactions are so ingrained into your psyche that you trigger your self-diminishing remarks and respond to them without an ounce of your conscious effort. Meditation allows you to become a kind of external observer in your own head and rediscover what's going through your mind.

This effect is as fast as it is strong. People who meditate for just a few days start to notice their own thought and behavior patterns in the middle of the day, several hours after their meditation session. Because they are aware of them, they can change the automatic impulse-response reaction.

In the space between stimulus (what happens) and how we respond, lies our freedom to choose. Ultimately, this power to choose is what defines us as human beings. We may have limited choices but we can always choose.
– Stephen R. Covey

This is how people become more productive after meditation. They spot their procrastination routines and modify their behavior. This is how stress level declines. People notice their hot buttons and can avoid them or soften their reactions.

And this is how you will finally be able to see what's coming when your subconscious throws a vicious insult at you the next time.

You need to see the opponent to fight him (unless you are Arya Stark, of course). You need to be aware of your self-talk before you can modify it or step in between the stimulus and your own reaction.

ACTION PLAN

1. **Start small.**

   If you've never meditated, two minutes is more than enough for a start.

2. **Take care of your environment.**

   Meditation is best served in peace and quiet. Be alone. Sit comfortably. Close your eyes.

   Sometimes the flow of time is different while meditating, so setting up an alarm clock is not a bad idea.

3. **Don't overthink the details.**

   Whether you are alone or not, which sitting position you choose, and even whether to close your eyes are secondary considerations. I've meditated with my eyes open on crowded subway trains huddled between co-passengers. When you're first getting started, being someplace quiet and closing your eyes can help you stay focused, which is why I recommend this above. But it isn't vital to do it this way.

The same is true about the length of your sessions. If you can meditate for five minutes without a problem, ignore my advice about two-minute sessions. If even two minutes frustrates you, try just three deep breaths at a time.

How you meditate is of little importance as long as you, indeed, meditate.

CHAPTER 5

THE POWER OF SILENCE

Being silent is another first-level method you can employ in your quest to improve your internal dialog. Its main advantage over meditation is that it is very easily measurable. You either said something or you didn't. You don't need to second-guess yourself, which happens many times with meditation: "Have I done it right or not?" Here, the output is very clear: either you kept your mouth shut and that's success or you didn't, and you know you messed up. You can also measure the time you were silent.

Silence also feels more natural than meditation for most. Too often, when people attempt to meditate for the first time, they feel that it is something "woo-woo." It's absolutely not. You close your eyes and breathe. How can it be unnatural or magical? But whatever you think becomes your reality, and thus many people are simply uncomfortable with meditation.

Silence is a source of great strength.
– Lao Tzu

There is no more down-to-earth activity than being silent, not speaking. It happens all the time in your life. Even the most talkative people are silent from time to time. You just need to use this state more purposefully.

Of course, this method might be easier for introverts. Talkers can struggle with keeping their mouth shut for an extended period. For the 50% of the population that are extroverts, silence is slightly harder to practice than meditation.

THE MIND-TONGUE MOTORWAY

But what does silence have to do with your self-talk? Your outward talk and your self-talk are closely connected. Whatever you speak out loud, you have to first think in your head. You may not realize it because usually the flow of words is seamless. You think something, and it appears automatically on your tongue.

I call this connection the mind-tongue motorway. It's two directional. What you say out loud affects what you say in your head, as well, but the connection in this direction is not instantaneous nor as influential. I imagine the mind-tongue motorway as having ten lanes from your mind to your tongue and one lane from your tongue to your mind. This is aptly designed for the requirements of your word traffic. Everything you say must emerge from your mind, but only a fraction of what you say is used as input for your thinking processes.

Now, guess what happens when you shut down ten lanes of a motorway? You are absolutely right: a horrible traffic jam!

If you shut down the motorway, all your thoughts will be imprisoned in your head with no easy way out. They will bounce around. They will mill around. The thoughts that you habitually blurt out without a second thought will stay inside your skull. If you diligently keep your silence when someone addresses you with a question or remark, you will learn the basics of self-talk control.

If you can't utter a word, your response will be different than the automatic status quo. Maybe you will decide it is worth it to breach your wall of silence, but it will be a conscious decision, a result of your reflection, not the usual automatic reply.

You will also notice how much of what you habitually say is simply unnecessary. If you are like most human beings, it comes straight from your ego.

I practiced silence for several months. The end goal of this practice for me was to be completely silent the whole of an average day. I never managed to achieve that; my low was about twenty sentences. But I noticed how very often I spoke only to be noticed, recognized, or appreciated. A lot of vicious internal dialog comes from the same place. You want to be part of a tribe and as soon as you feel you don't belong, your insecurities start to emerge.

The result of your silence practice is very similar to the goal of meditation: an increased self-awareness about your self-talk. Imprison your dialog in your head, cut it off so it's not released habitually, and you will become more mindful about what goes through your head.

I believe my success with adopting the meditation habit was probably because of my silence practice. My self-awareness was already high enough that I wasn't alarmed by the crowd of uninvited thoughts running through my mind when I tried to focus on my breathing.

SPIRITUAL AND TANGIBLE BENEFITS

Again, this kind of self-awareness is fundamental for your progress. You cannot improve or fix something you are not aware of. Only if you notice your unwanted thoughts can you do something about them. If they attack you and put you into a habitual vicious loop of self-talk, you will be helpless forever. If you see what's coming, you can break the loop and change the output.

There is nothing woo-woo in the silence practice, nothing mystical, it's very tangible. Shut up. That's all. No affirmation, no wishful thinking, no sending your vibrations to the universe involved. Just be quiet.

I study saints and many of them were members of Catholic religious orders that have the practice of silence written as a law in their monastic rules. Saint Alfonse Luguori has a whole Chapter about the importance of silence in his book *The Way of Salvation and of Perfection*. In the Bible, an empty talkativeness is often discouraged if not downright condemned.

> *If the fool holds his tongue, he may pass for wise;*
> *if he seals his lips, he may pass for intelligent.*
> – Proverbs, 17: 28

There is little wisdom or meekness in talking too much, exactly as there is little wisdom and true meekness in uncontrolled self-talk.

As with everything else in the modern world, silence has been the subject of much scientific research. Scientists have concluded that it's beneficial for our health—it lowers blood pressure, boosts the body's immune system, decreases stress by lowering blood cortisol levels and adrenaline, promotes good hormone regulation, and prevents plaque formation in the arteries.

A 2013 study found that two hours of silence could create new brain cells in the hippocampus region, and a study from 2006 concluded that two minutes of silence relieves tension in the body and brain and is more relaxing than listening to music.

Scientists connected silence with increased creativity, better cognitive abilities, and relief from insomnia.

STEER THE TRAFFIC OF YOUR WORDS

The silence practice is not restricted to unconditional muteness for the whole day. You can practice it in many variations, and they all will provide similar benefits. Of course, the more restrictive your practice is, the faster you will get its benefits and the greater those benefits will be. But you can manipulate your silence discipline in any way you wish to and still reap the benefits.

I know how uncomfortable and difficult (bordering on impossible) it is to not say a word for the whole day. You live in a society. You interact with your spouse, children, workmates, and many other people. Thus, you can limit your silence practice to only specific times in your schedule, for example during your commute to work. Or you can arrange your work to provide an hour-long break with no words in the middle of your workday. Obviously, this won't happen during the part of your day when you attend meetings, right?

You can place different restrictions on your mind-tongue motorway. Allow yourself to speak only a specific number of times per hour. Or give yourself a limit of words or sentences you can use in one hour or one day.

These methods are more adapted to the normal lifestyle—you cannot be a freak who says nothing all the time—but at the same time they're harder to practice. All or nothing is easy to track.

Giving yourself permission to say something suggests some rules you have to keep track of. It's easier to fall off the wagon and even easier to say to yourself: "Oh, I forgot about this and talked too much. Well, I'll start again tomorrow." And the "tomorrow" keeps getting pushed to tomorrow.

But the benefits of those modified tactics are very similar to the full-muteness practice, and in some ways even better. If you have to think about what you are saying, you utilize both directions of the mind-tongue motorway. You have to ponder what you are going to say to stay within your limit of words or utterances, and you need to track what you are actually saying. You both think about what to say and listen to yourself while saying it.

Because you pay more attention to your speech patterns, your self-awareness will increase more rapidly, and it will be stronger. The most amazing thing is that you will actually get some grip over your self-talk in the process. If you can govern your tongue, you gain control over your self-talk to some degree. The same automatic mechanisms that make you blurt things out trigger your inward blurts. If you can affect one, you can affect another.

Thus, "partial silence" is the first exercise that will actually make a direct difference in what you say to yourself and how you respond to your subconscious prods.

ACTION PLAN

1. **Choose and implement a silence practice. You can mix them or trim them to your needs and circumstances.**

    A. *Enter full-muteness practice.*

        If possible, try to shut up for the whole day. It may be a day off or a day spent working on a solo project.

        If not possible, restrict full-muteness to a specific period of time. One hour seems to be a nice round number. Or you can pick a shorter period in a more challenging period, for example, ten minutes during the morning rush.

        The whole beauty of this practice lies in its simplicity. You cannot utter a word. Period.

        You can still communicate, but without speaking. When I silenced myself, I used gestures and grunts extensively.

B. *Set restrictions to your speech.*

Allow yourself one sentence per ten minutes or a dozen words per hour or three interactions per two hours.

The specific plan must be yours, adjusted to your circumstances. If you work in customer service, it's close to impossible to expect that you will be silent at work. If your kiddo just learned the magic word "Why?" saying nothing is not an option.

C. *Mix muteness and restrictions.*

This is the moderate middle way. Set yourself for complete muteness, but give yourself some backdoors: "If someone calls..." "If there is a meeting..." "If a client arrives..."

That way you will reap the benefits of imprisoning words in your head while giving yourself permission to "fail" from time to time.

2. **Track your discipline.**

When I tried to be quiet for the whole day, I tracked how many times I breached the silence. I simply jotted a stroke in my notepad whenever I said something.

Silence is very easy to track. You either said nothing or you said something. Come up with some system to record one or both situations. A pen and notepad, an app, or even a mark on your wall calendar—any method is fine as long as it suits you. Keep it simple and effective.

CHAPTER 6

THE POWER OF GRATITUDE

Gradually we arrive at the more difficult methods, which will have more impact on your internal dialog. The three disciplines I talk about in this and the next two Chapters are very tangible and down to earth. They also modify your self-talk directly. It's now less about self-awareness and more about speaking to yourself in a better manner.

The first method is gratitude journaling. You just write down a few things you are grateful for. These "things" can be practically anything. You can be grateful for your possessions, your history, the people you live or work with, the wonders of nature, events in your life or your close ones' lives, interactions with friends, your health, or your bank account balance—there are no limits.

The biggest obstacle in doing this is mental, not physical. It's super easy to do. In the minimum version, you need to write only three bullet points. It shouldn't take you more than a couple of minutes and will usually probably take less than thirty seconds. If you can write, you are good to go.

But many people are suspicious of this activity because "it's not what normal people do." Normal people also have really crappy self-talk. You don't want to be normal in that way, do you? Get rid of the feeling that writing down things you are grateful for is some-how silly. Is your health, marriage, or bank account balance silly? This practice will have direct positive impact on those three items and more, as I will explain further in this Chapter.

So, how do you keep a gratitude journal? Follow this formula for the best results:

- Write your entries in the journal by hand
- Do it in the morning to positively frame your day
- Note down at least three new things every time
- Elaborate on your entries: think of the reasons for or the specifics of your gratitude

If you want to know the ins and outs of this formula and the research backing it, take a look at this 3,000-word article I wrote on the subject: https://medium.com/personal-growth/how-a-one-minute-action-changed-my-life-completely-68c1a699e587

YOU AREN'T REALISTIC, YOU ARE NEGATIVE

People have a huge negativity bias. We focus more easily on the unpleasant side of life than on the positive. Nobody really knows why, but it's a well-established fact. It is why the news is full of negative information—we pay more attention to negativity. If they didn't spread negativity, they would go bankrupt.

Some speculate that negativity bias comes from prehistoric times when our ancestors had to be constantly on their toes, looking for the signs of dangers, natural catastrophes, or carnivores. But nowadays we don't need to worry much about starvation or being attacked by a bear, so the negativity bias has turned inward.

Instead of searching for a tiger lurking in high grass, your brain searches for social cues in your environment and "warns" you against social dangers. Your spouse didn't react with a joyful outburst when you told a joke, your kid sulked when you tried to gently correct his behavior, your boss angrily threw a stack of papers on your desk. You constantly wonder what others think of you. All those signals probably mean there is something wrong with you! And your self-talk goes crazy.

Another theory is that people developed this mechanism of self-talk and negativity bias to correct themselves. If you were submissive and cooperative, you got along well with your tribe. If you were an unlikable arrogant prick, it was a death sentence because a lone human had no chance of survival.

No matter the original reason, the fact is that you think a lot about yourself and your social interactions, and you look for signs of danger rather than signs of acceptance. That's why your internal dialog is concerned mostly with what you did wrong and how bad of a person you are.

The good news is that this default mode is reversible. You are not the first one with this specific problem.

> *If anyone else has done it, you can do it,*
> *and if someone else hasn't done it, you can do it first.*
> – Jeremy Frandsen's grandma

The above quote may be overly optimistic. I can't imagine myself winning a gold medal at the Olympics in tennis, despite the fact that quite a few of people have achieved this before.

The good news is that when it comes to self-talk, it's *not* overly optimistic, and you won't be the first one. Countless millions of people have been able to shape their self-talk in a more positive way. That's not a rare skill or talent. It's available for everybody, including yourself.

> *Gratitude rewires the human brain into positivity.*
> – Shawn Achor

This is the end result you seek from practicing this discipline. The cool thing about a gratitude journal is that it is a proven way to achieve this result. And it's pretty powerful.

For a mind-blowing example, let's look at a five-year-old with a pessimism gene and an eighty-year-old with the same gene.

When scientists researched the kiddo, they wanted to find out if this simple discipline of gratitude journaling could overcome genetic conditions. It could and within only thirty days! So they found an old guy with the same gene who had lived in his grumpy ways for eighty years. Within thirty days of beginning a gratitude journal, his brain was rewired into positivity as well.

You don't have any tangible excuses. Neither your genes nor how you have functioned up until today is an obstacle for introducing gratitude into your life.

You can listen to a fascinating interview with a positive psychology researcher here if you are interested in more scientific details: https://www.entreleadership.com/podcasts/shawn-achorhow-happiness-fuels-your-suc

If you still don't believe the science, then just look at my results. I was grumpy. My life motto was: "Expect the worst, you will have only positive surprises." Nowadays, I'm sunshine; I'm oozing gratitude and positivity from every pore of my body. Well, at least compared to my previous state. My optimistic friends without genetic burden or who never had a negative outlook on life still beat me in optimism. ;)

GOOGLE IN YOUR HEAD

In reality, scientists have little clue why gratitude is such a powerful tool for positive conditioning. They've conducted experiments. They've measured brain activity with MRI imaging. They've observed the positive results. But I have yet to hear an explanation for why it works that way that wasn't pure speculation.

My guess is that the human brain is primarily a search engine. We have quite amazing abstract thinking abilities, and we can recall memories probably better than any other mammal, but those aren't the main functions of our brains.

Our brains process over eleven million sensory impulses every single second. This is more than a billion impulses in less than two minutes! And every second your brain filters this enormous amount of data to give your consciousness a targeted sample that is the most relevant to you. It's the most sophisticated search engine known to humanity. Our brains' other abilities are dwarfed by their ability to browse the enormous ocean of data and fish out only the truly important information.

The negativity bias makes your fishermen look for sharks. You focus on physical danger and, where there is a lack of it, on social danger. A focus on gratitude makes you search for good things in your life.

In effect, you change the default search filters in your search engine. The beauty of gratitude journaling is that it works well below your conscious level. You don't fight with your subconscious. You don't argue with it or try to force it to change course. You don't scream in your head: "Become positive, sucker!" It's like breaking into a server room and quietly overwriting the whole operation system of your brain. Your search engine starts to look for all kinds of good things in your life. It rewires into positivity.

As a result, your self-talk shifts. If your brain fishes out less excrement from your data ocean, it uses it less in your internal vocabulary. If it finds more good things and brings them to your conscious mind, more positivity appears in your self-talk. You can accelerate this process further by giving at least part of the space in your gratitude journal to things you did well.

I'm grateful for many different things, events, phenomena, and people in my life, but I also purposefully note down some of my small achievements every day. Whenever I move a project forward or stick to my daily disciplines, I put it in my gratitude journal as a reminder that I, indeed, did some things well.

Is gratitude journaling a super-duper almighty tool against negativity? As much as I want to scream "Yes!" it's not. It works amazingly well. Can you imagine any other one-minute activity that can change a grumpy old man into a cheerful person? But humans are amazingly creative creatures. We can screw up practically everything, including gratitude journaling.

The first way to mess it up is to insist on doing it your way rather than following the guidelines above and then claim it doesn't work. One of my coaching clients kept writing the same three things every day and was surprised that it didn't make him more positive.

In fact, making sure that you are writing at least three *new* things every day is the only ironclad rule among the above guidelines. You may modify the routine; you probably even *should*, so you own it in your head. It works best when you use your gratitude journal in the morning, write by hand, and elaborate on your entries, but none of those are crucial. You can write more entries. I don't write in the morning very often and rarely elaborate on my entries. I know a gal—my gratitude guru—who kept her entries in an online journal, so she types them.

Other methods of screwing up typically come from your self-talk getting in the way. People are amazingly creative, so I can't give you an example of every way this could go wrong. I will instance three specific cases that I have personally encountered to give you an idea.

"It's stupid."

You can have your own opinion. You can believe in pink unicorns or that gratitude journaling is stupid. This "argument" can dismiss practically everything. But this is just your opinion, not the facts.

The fact is that gratitude practice is not stupid, in the same way that reading and exercising are not stupid. It makes you a better person. Period. You can't claim otherwise, if you don't try it in the first place.

"I don't have much to be grateful for. I'll run out of ideas quickly."

I have practiced gratitude journaling for over five years. I have easily written down about 22,000 reasons for being grateful. Stick to three things a day. You will run out of ideas in about twenty years. But don't worry about it just now. For twenty years you will keep improving your life. Surely, you will figure something out when you reach the limit.

Jokes aside, this is not a valid worry. You will never run out of reasons for being grateful just like you will never run out of air to breathe unless you confine yourself in a space with a limited air supply. Neglecting gratitude journaling is like confining yourself to a mental space with limited gratitude supply.

"I'll jinx my own happiness."

You know, when you admit you have something to be grateful for, some evil force—an evil universe, Satan, demons, an evil tooth fairy, the bogeyman—will snatch it from you and you will be miserable again.

sigh

How can I discuss such an argument? It's irrational, so pointing out logical holes in this kind of thinking won't be of much use. I'll try nonetheless. First of all, why does this evil force need your admission to snatch goodness from your life? If the universe is against you, you have no chance anyway, no matter what you do or admit.

If you are afraid of Satan, you should put your trust in God. If you believe in one, you have to believe in the other too. And only one of them is Almighty and loves you.

If an evil tooth fairy gives you sleepless nights, get real. In the end "jinxing" is a fear in your head that things will never get better for you. It's so paralyzing, that you come up with wild stories that allow you to do nothing. That is the intention of this jinxing narration going on in your head—doing nothing.

Here is the uncomfortable secret: if you do nothing, certainly things cannot get better for you. Doing nothing is maintaining the status quo and it never lasts for too long. If you don't actively try to improve your life, it will probably deteriorate, and this process will be more rapid the longer you passively sit on your butt.

Action is the best remedy to the stories in your head. Whether you think it's stupid or you worry you will jinx your luck, or whatever else, debating those arguments in your head is a losing proposition. If you could talk yourself out of self-damaging ideas, you wouldn't need this book. You will gain this ability with practice, but right now JUST DO IT. Sit your butt down, take a pen, and write three things you are grateful for.

Done.

Rinse and repeat.

GRATITUDE EQUALS RESULTS

Do I sound a bit preachy about this subject? Probably because I am. I've experienced the power of gratitude in my life firsthand, and it blows my mind that people don't practice it. There is so much more to this practice than feeling good or "attracting happiness." I'm a down-to-earth person. Gratitude journaling brings results. All kinds of them. It brings them quickly, in measurable, statistically significant form.

At the beginning of this Chapter I quoted Shawn Achor about gratitude rewiring the human brain into positivity. This is his quote about the effects of positivity on your life:

> *When the brain is positive, every possible outcome we know*
> *how to test for raises dramatically.*
> – Shawn Achor

Scientists tested for everything they could think of measuring. Health, relationships, sales, grades at school, bank account balance, fitness performance, chances of promotion at work— everything!

There was no single exception. I guess there never will be one. It's a law of nature. When your brain is positive, you get better results in everything.

Self-talk is only one of many facets of your life that will improve if you keep a gratitude journal. Some other aspects of your life directly related to self-talk will improve as well, like positive self-awareness, self-control, or mindfulness.

And your whole life will get better! Wouldn't it be great to lose 10% of your excess weight, have 15% more friends, 5% more money in your bank account, and 10% fewer worries with a snap of your fingers? Gratitude journal is not quite so magical; it takes about thirty days to rewire your brain into positivity and only then the effect kicks in. But unlike a snap of your fingers, this practice *will* give you all of these results and more.

I heard Shawn Achor on a podcast when I had been keeping a gratitude journal for three years. I enjoyed doing it, but I didn't pay much attention to it. It was just a fun thing to do for me. Then I listened to this podcast episode and realized that a huge part of my success in the previous three years could be credited to the positivity of my brain, which was maintained thanks to my gratitude journals.

In three years, I turned from a miserable employee with no real purpose in life into a passionate author following a well-defined personal mission. Everything in my life got better. From my spiritual life to my possessions, my life was better in every aspect. I prayed more, got sick significantly fewer times, increased my savings ratio, beat dozens of personal fitness records, earned more, got more friends, and so on. I could continue this list for the next ten thousand words.

But what if I could credit only 15% of all those results to my gratitude journals? This still qualifies as "dramatic." It more than justifies this tiny activity, in my eyes.

By the way, Achor is a scientist, and he talks about tangible, measurable metrics. My experience is that "every outcome" means truly *everything*, including things unmeasurable to science. I mentioned my spiritual life. The same goes for my self-confidence, vulnerability, authenticity, happiness, and many other aspects of my life that are hard to define or measure.

So, please, write down three things you are grateful for right now. Start fixing your life.

ACTION PLAN

1. **Start a gratitude journal—right now!**

    Use any recording medium available—a mobile, pen and paper, a word processor on your computer. Again, the medium is secondary. I prefer pen and paper because scientific studies confirm that handwriting creates more associations than typing.

    The perfect recipe is:

    "Every morning, write three new things you are grateful for."

    By "things" I mean anything: your spouse, the weather, some bodily sensation, the beauty of nature, your talents, possessions, friends, what you got from others, what you give to others. Anything.

    It's beneficial to do it in the morning to positively frame your day, but it's not crucial. You don't have to restrict yourself to three entries, it's just the minimal requirement. However, coming up with new reasons for being grateful is the core of this method. It trains your brain to look for positives.

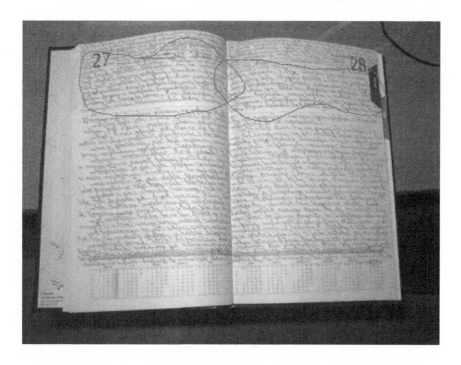

2. Track.

Once you start your journal, tracking is self-explanatory. You either have your three entries in the journal or not.

CHAPTER 7

THE POWER OF JOURNALING

In the previous Chapter, I beat the concept of gratitude journaling to death. This Chapter is dedicated to journaling in general. I consider it harder to do. It's the first method that is impossible to do without some basic resources. You can meditate on the fly or jot down three reasons for being grateful in less than a minute. Real journaling cries for more time, and time is the required resource to do it right. It's also the resource most of us feel incredibly short of.

But there is no way around this. If you want to keep a real journal, you need to block out time for that. It's not just a matter of finding the time. You need the *right* time, when you can find a few minutes of peace and quiet and be alone with your thoughts. You can journal on the fly only to a degree.

In fact, part of the point of this practice is to force you to reserve some time and focus. To journal, you need to use your mind in a way that is not matter-of-fact, so you need some quiet, solitary time for this. I journal in the morning when everybody else at my home is asleep. No one interrupts me. I dedicate ten to twenty minutes every day for journaling. I think five minutes should be a minimum you reserve for this discipline.

Time-investment is a downside of this method, but it has its upsides too. The foremost one is that you won't feel uneasy when doing general journaling, as you might when meditating or gratitude journaling. Journaling is a socially accepted activity and few people label it weird or stupid. Many prominent figures in Western history journaled, such as Marcus Aurelius, the famous Roman Emperor; Napoleon Bonaparte; and Benjamin Franklin.

How do you think journaling is viewed? Social considerations inhabit your mind too. It's one thing to try some activity you consider semi-magical and overcome your subconscious resistance against it. It's entirely different to start an activity you can be persuaded is almost mainstream.

Another advantage of journaling is that it leaves a track record. It's tangible. After each journaling session you have a sheet of paper, or a few of them, covered with words. You can touch it, you can smell it, you can reread your notes and reflect about them. This is doubly beneficial: first, you get a tangible weapon against your subconscious and its vicious self-talk; second, it speaks to our materialistic philosophy.

Make no mistake, compared to medieval people, we are a highly materialistic society. This impacts your personal philosophy. Nowadays we value things that can be seen, touched, and measured. And we are suspicious of anything that cannot be weighed and exists only as a conviction about a principle.

Even if you are more spiritually inclined than most, you are continually bombarded by the materialistic point of view, simply because you live in our current society. Again, it comes down to your subconscious feeling about the activity and decreasing the internal resistance.

THE SUBJECT MATTER: YOU

What should you write about in your journal? I prescribe self-reflections. This is what I'm using my journaling for in the most part. It is good to block some time to think about yourself in a way you are not used to.

Gratitude journaling is self-reflective but only in a narrow way. When you get really introspective, you don't ask only about what you are grateful for, but also:

- what are your dreams and ambitions?
- what are you afraid of?
- what you are passionate about?
- what holds you back?
- how do you want to overcome your obstacles?
- what are your plans?
- who do you want to become?
- why do you feel the way you feel?
- ... and so on.

I ask myself an insightful question and answer it on paper. On the seventh day, I read and review my entries. I've been doing it since 26th of May, 2013. If you need prompts for your journaling, sign-up to receive 100 questions straight from my journals: www.expandbeyondyourself.com/powerup-journal

Self-talk is a controlling mechanism that whips you like an animal; your responses to this are animalistic, automatic. But you are not a beast. When your "master" with his whip is away, you can write down what's happening inside you. You can use the language of your conscious mind—words—and avoid the language of your subconscious mind, which is emotions.

However, self-reflection is not obligatory. In the end you need to add your own flavor to every habit I recommend, or you will abandon it. You need to write what you want to write about, not what I force on you. When building any habit, sustainability is the most important thing. Your journaling cannot feel imposed on you, or you will give up sooner rather than later.

Having said that, keep in mind what Eleanor Roosevelt once said:

Great minds discuss ideas; average minds discuss events;
small minds discuss people.

Don't write about everyday trivia. Don't dwell on your petty feelings, how someone hurt you, what your spouse or workmate told you, or how offensively they behaved. Don't write how awesome the latest episode of *Games of Thrones* was. Avoid emotion-based reflections; steer your journaling into the realm of ideas and events.

Emotions will appear in your journal anyway. They appear very often in my journal, but most of the time in pursuit of self-discovery: Why the heck did I feel like that? What in the world made me lose my temper like that? What can I do in the future to avoid such outbursts? How can I change my petty behavior into something constructive?

My journals are full of my dreams, fears, aspirations, plans for improvement, business ideas, to-do items for next month, book ideas, and my spiritual growth.

Most of those things are high-level ideas, but there is a plenty of accompanying emotional drama that gets spilled on paper when I write about those ideas.

If you want to write about events, shift them into the ideas realm. For example, when you watch a debate on TV about some controversial topic that polarizes public opinion, like abortion, gay marriage, or gun control, you can write down your opinion about the events and your rationale for having that opinion. How has your opinion been shaped over time? What influenced it?

What makes journaling so powerful in improving your internal debate? Foremost, you use words, which are the language of your conscious mind. You start using logic more and emotions less. The debate on paper is less about emotional allusions and intuition and more about facts. Once recorded, the slippery eel of your thoughts is no longer wriggling about in your mind. Your arguments have been outed. It's like taking your internal arguments from the home of your mind to a courthouse.

Everything gets recorded. Everything gets a meaning. You cannot un-tell invectives or self-loathing thoughts on paper. Your subconscious cannot pretend that "it has meant something else." For ten or fifteen minutes of journaling, you get control over the steering wheel of your mind. This may be a totally new and liberating experience for you.

Instead of reacting to arriving thoughts, like a tennis player who hits incoming balls, you can take over the process. You can use the pause between the arrival of a thought and writing it down to create a gap for your action, not just for emotional reaction.

For me, journaling feels like actually doing something. When I meditate, I cannot help but feel idle. When I'm scribbling my thoughts down, it feels like a proper activity. So, I feel better in the process. And the end result is very similar. I had been practicing journaling for one year before I started meditation. I didn't meet with the initial resistance of many first-time meditators. I wasn't overwhelmed by the constant chatter in my head that revealed itself when I tried to focus on simple body functions. I was used to it. My journaling sessions were full of observing this chatter and registering it on paper.

I was aware of my subconscious impulses.

SELF-TALK ON PAPER

When you capture your thoughts on paper, the output is chaotic, but less chaotic than you might think. This is the benefit of writing—you need to process your emotions through words and it makes the output at least moderately clear. It's no longer a muddy mix of emotions, reactions, and some words. It's a narration.

This narration reveals quite a lot about your subconscious. First of all, it shows you how dumb it is. If you read your self-talk frozen in words on paper, you see that the arguments are weak, if not downright stupid. It's often like a dialog with a stubborn kid. "You are stupid!" and "Because I don't want to!" seem like the most sophisticated arguments of your inner self.

Insults and pouts may be effective when they are used inside your mind, but on paper they look ridiculous. Other discoveries follow this realization. You realize that most of your actions are steered by this stubborn kid... and you let that happen. You realize that your subconscious is very powerful; that's *why* you let that happen. Subconscious mind knows only the present moment, so each argument is fresh for it. It will never get tired of repeating the same signals that provided results in the past.

However, thanks to journaling, you can win the debate. You are like a parent who patiently explains logical arguments to a kid. When a kiddo stops driving his agenda and starts to argue to a parent with logic, he must accept the logic in the end.

The same goes with journaling. If you take the debate to your territory, if you capture self-talk in words, you rob your subconscious of its most effective weapon—emotions. Emotions can bring you down very quickly. Sometimes it seems to be their only purpose. Self-loathing, self-doubts, and passivity are not the results of facts, but of your feelings about those facts.

Emotions are not eliminated by the process of journaling. They are translated into words so you can see through them. Shame, regret, or grief are mostly the tools to make you submissive. When you see that clearly, you can do something about it.

When you think, *"What a shame! I failed! I don't want even to try anymore! I'm no good! That's a waste of time,"* it's not a discussion about facts but emotional bombardment that makes you passive. In your head, this train of thought can make sense. Captured on paper, it's a different story. You immediately see that if you stop trying, you cannot succeed. It's impossible.

You see that some real output—a failure—causes disproportional imaginary attachment to your self-worth. So what that you've failed? All people fail all the time! It's like saying: *"The sun came up! I'm no good!"*

In short, you can turn on your rational thinking via journaling.

ACTION PLAN

1. **Don't overwhelm yourself.**

   If you are a novice at journaling, don't start too ambitiously. Nowadays, I am a journaling machine, but I started from a single entry about my wife in a gratitude journal. For over three months, it was the only journaling activity I performed daily.

   On the other hand, I suggest you do as much as you can. The more data you "input," and the more commitment you make, the faster you will see results out of this discipline. Currently, I spend about half an hour a day on journaling.

2. **Start the journal you want to sustain.**

   The value from journaling comes principally over time. The more you do it, the more you'll get from it. Thus, you should start in a way you'll want to continue.

You have to enjoy the process. It's a must when you begin journaling. It can't be yet another chore on your to-do list. You don't need more of them, do you?

You don't *have* to like journaling, but liking any new habit will help you maintain it. My most time-consuming habit is writing 600 words a day six days a week and at least 400 words on Sundays. Trust me—I don't always enjoy writing my 600 words. Sometimes it's more of a chore than a pleasure, but I can maintain it.

3. **Protect your time.**

Whether your journaling session takes you three minutes or one, you need to reserve your time for it.

I journal in the morning, when my family is still asleep. That way I'm sure no one will interrupt me.

You may pick another time of the day. Maybe the evening when everybody is already asleep. Maybe a lunch break. Picking the same time every day will speed up developing a journaling habit... and you need to block time for it anyway.

4. **Review your journal regularly.**

You should review your journal from time to time. Just recording your experiences and reflections will increase your self-knowledge and self-awareness. However, reading and reflecting on your notes will greatly speed up this process.

CHAPTER 8

THE POWER OF YOUR WORDS

In 2016, research at Ohio State University examined more than 266,000 writing samples provided by 2342 minimum-security inmates in therapy programs. The researchers concluded that the more prisoners had changed their linguistic habits by the time they were released, the more likely they were to stay out of jail.

Your vocabulary is like a gate for your mindset. It may be narrow and restricted or wide and open. Widening your worldview is very important, but it's just one aspect of enriching your vocabulary. Another is that you simply give raw material to your mind. It's like how the questions you ask yourself determine what your answers will be. If you ask yourself: "Why am I such a failure?" your brain will happily provide you answers. It's what it was designed for.

When Jim Rohn, business philosopher and one of the best American speakers, discovered the results of his friends' survey among prisoners in New England (they worked on a rehabilitation program), he wasn't surprised by their conclusions: The more limited the vocabulary, the greater the tendency to poor behavior. Jim marveled about this discovery:

"Vocabulary is a way of seeing. One reason for vocabulary is to inter-pret what we see, to interpret what we hear. [...]

If you've got a poor set of words and skills and tools with which to interpret, you can imagine the errors and the mistakes you'll make in judgment."

Of course, if you are partially or completely blind, you stumble and struggle. What is more, errors from your blindness compound with time and make your life even harder.

Your vocabulary works on a deep, subtle level. When your brain forms answers, it uses what it knows. It queries from the set of available words to express the meaning. If you provide more words, your brain will have a wider palette of possible options.

It doesn't mean it will automatically use them. However, if you don't add new words to your vocabulary, you are guaranteed you will never hear them in your internal dialog.

Compared to all the previous methods, working on your vocab-ulary is a tedious matter. This is like any big habit you try to develop. It fully occupies your conscious mind, especially at the beginning. You need to control what you are thinking, at least periodically, and thinking is the hardest work in the world.

But it's worth it. You've surely heard the expression "No pain no gain" before, haven't you? Yes, the effort here is much bigger than in the previous methods. However, the gains are also bigger, faster, and better. So why am I introducing this method at the end? Exactly *because* it's harder to do than the others. You need to first learn to walk before you run. You needed increased self-awareness to be able to attempt struggles with your vocabulary.

Modifying your vocabulary in a proper way takes lot of mind-fulness or painstaking tracking (which results in even greater mindfulness). I definitely prefer tracking, even though many find it a pain in the butt. Like with journaling, tracking your progress takes the battle out of your mind. Smoke and mirrors of the mind are the home ground of the subconscious. If you try to be aware of your words only by being mindful about them, your subconscious can cunningly trick you into thinking that you are doing a great job, when in fact you aren't.

TRACK YOUR WORDS

Normal people simply don't have sufficient self-awareness to consciously know what they are saying all the time.

Hence, instead of constantly trying to be mindful about the words you use, it's much easier and effective to track this usage on paper or in an application.

Yes, we all have the ability to think whatever we choose to, but it is not developed. It's like a baby's power over the movement of her hands. She can move them, that's a given, but there is little control over those movements, especially at the beginning.

Tracking will create mindfulness. You will practice self-awareness and with time it will get easier, more automatic. A baby finally learns to control her limbs by constant practice. Tracking will be your practice.

In the end, your self-awareness about your vocabulary may be as automatic as a child's control over her arms and hands. Tracking creates subconscious routines in your brain. It's not a theory.

When I worked on losing excess weight at the beginning of 2013, I jotted down everything I consumed that contained calories (so only water was exempted from my tracking). It was a difficult discipline to develop and irritating to maintain. Every time I put something in my mouth, I immediately wrote it down. And I consumed a lot, so I often wrote it down on sticky notes. Then, whenever I was at the computer, I rewrote my notes to a text file. It was annoying.

Soon, I bypassed part of this process. I kept my consumption in my head and dumped it to a text file whenever I was at the computer. My periods of keeping the consumption in my mind got extended and extended. After a few weeks, I tracked my consumption in my head and didn't write it in the file until the evening, when I knew I wouldn't eat or drink anything more.

I carried in my head everything I consumed from dusk till dawn, and I registered it in the digital journal at the end of the day. And I created a habit. My food tracking lasted about nine weeks before I reached my dream weight. Then I quit the discipline.

However, over five years later, I still can remember what I've consumed from dusk till dawn. It doesn't involve even an ounce of my conscious mind. Whenever I want, I can recall everything I ate and drank to the smallest detail. I don't have to look for this information, don't have to sweat to remember it. It's conveniently stored in the cache of my memory. But don't ask me what I ate yesterday. This information is purged from my memory cache overnight. I have to recall it like any other memory.

GOVERN YOUR TONGUE

Introducing new words into your vocabulary will also use the mind-tongue motorway. Silence creates a traffic jam on this motorway. Modifying your vocabulary will give you the first taste of controlling this traffic. Maybe for the first time in your life, you will be in charge of at least one lane of your mind-tongue motorway. And that's the goal of this book, to put the reins of your self-talk into your hands. Well, it's a bit like getting the reins of the elephant you are riding. Pure brute force won't do you much good. But you will get at least some measure of control. It's better to sit on an elephant and clutch the reins than sit on it and have no means of control at all.

Ironically, your adventure with vocabulary will be easier to start if you think first about eliminating words you no longer want. When you try to introduce something new into your mind, it's easy to lose track, to let it slip from your mind and simply forget. Then at the end of your day you look at your tracking sheet and think: *"Heck, I completely forgot to say this new word even once today!"*

However, when you focus on not saying something, it's much better for your self-awareness. Cussing is a widespread bad habit. If you decide to stop cussing, it's so easy to fail and instinctively use an f-bomb when something gets on your nerves. But it is also almost impossible not to notice your slip.

Eliminating words from your vocabulary is miraculously effective for self-awareness about your speech patterns.

Unfortunately, you cannot expect a high success rate. It's hard to break habits that have been forming for years and decades. The odds are stacked against you. Don't worry. With this technique you aim for practice rather than success. It's the discipline of focusing on what goes through your mouth that will build your self-talk awareness muscle.

Of course, there is a danger of giving your negative self-talk too much leeway with this discipline, because the number of failures can be frustrating and discouraging. Frustration and discouragement are like fertilizer for negativity. To avoid that, start small. Try not to cuss (or use a specific word you want to avoid) only for ten minutes or one hour or before noon or after you are back from work. It's easier to maintain focus for a limited time and actually succeed with tongue control.

The same goes with introducing new words into your vocabulary. Instead of trying to force yourself to say your new word all the time, start by committing to use it three times during the whole day. Or focus on saying it once in the next fifteen minutes. Or think in advance about a situation in your day when you can use this word and focus only on saying the word in this situation. The point is to start really small.

By the way, by "words," I mean both single words and expressions you want to include in your everyday language. You don't need to limit yourself to single verbs, nouns, or adjectives.

One more thing: the words you introduce don't have to be completely new to you. I'm talking about using the words in everyday situations, not just knowing they exist. If you use the word "fabulous" once in a blue moon, you can resolve to use it ten times a day. That's another way to start small and with less internal friction.

You also don't want to simply repeat the word like an affirmation or mantra: "fabulous, fabulous, fabulous, fabulous..." It won't especially hurt if you do this, but it also won't be especially helpful. The only direct benefit will be to get some more associations to the word. You could write yourself a mantra, using a word or expression you want to use more often, but repeating mantras will not change your regular speech. Your goal should be to slowly change your everyday language. You'll only get the feedback-loop effect in your self-talk when new words are fully assimilated into your vocabulary.

Use new words and expressions in normal conversations; that's the key to smuggling them into your speech for good. It's one thing to use a fancy word during a work presentation, something you might only be called on to do once a quarter. It's quite something else to adopt the word as your own and use it habitually when you talk to your spouse, kids, or workmates.

ACTION PLAN

1. **Start with elimination**

   - pick one word you want to erase from your vocabulary
   - track each time you were not attentive enough and you blurted it out anyway
   - if you fail too often and it encourages negative self-talk, change the rules to be more favorable: reduce the time during which you must avoid the word, or mark your strategy a success if you avoid using it at least once in an hour.

2. Move to addition

- pick one word or expression
- try to use this word in normal conversations ten times a day (this an arbitrary metric; you can decide to use it two or two hundred times a day)
- variant: set a time limit, for example an hour, and try to use the world as soon as possible or as many times as possible during this period

You can play with different words each day. You can mingle or mix elimination and addition. The key to success is constant practice. And success is defined by the change of tone in your self-talk not by reaching your goals with elimination or addition of words. They are just milestones. Your ultimate goal here is to speak to yourself in a more civilized manner.

CHAPTER 9

THE POWER OF PLANNING

I'm now supposed to provide you a success blueprint for fixing your self-talk. It's an impossible task. Each of us is different. Each of us has their own type of struggle with their self-talk. There is no one-size-fits-all solution.

But I've done impossible things in the past, so I don't shy away from this challenge.

There is one rule that is absolutely universal in your quest for better self-talk: Do not ever stop. Never ever. No matter what. You need to keep going. You shall keep going. You must keep going. You have to.

The moment a thought about quitting your improvement of your self-talk crosses your mind, you are doomed. This option doesn't exist. It's mental suicide.

Your internal voice never stops. It generates constant chatter in your mind. It's a physiological activity, like breathing.

I think, therefore I am.

This may or may not be true; philosophers have a hard time deciding. But the opposite is certainly true: You are, therefore you think. Being and thinking are two inseparable activities for humans.

You will be stuck with the voice in your head for the rest of your life. Thus, you cannot ever stop trying to live on better terms with this voice. If you quit, you give up control over your life. In order to change yourself and your life, you need to take action and sustain it.

You need to persist in your quest for improved self-talk just as much as you persist in breathing.

I purposefully provided techniques that may and should be habitualized. Your internal discussion is constant and habitual. So should be the methods to improve it. Only if you make those methods part of your normal lifestyle will you be able to face your subconscious' vicious whispers. This is a full-time job and the tools I gave you will help you to make a permanent change.

RULE NUMBER ONE: NEVER GIVE UP

If you don't design your own life plan, chances are you'll fall into someone else's plan. And guess what they have planned for you? Not much.
– Jim Rohn

No one can replace you in this task. You can get only limited help from others. It's not like someone can get into your head and support you in deflecting self-limiting beliefs or verbal abuse from your inner self.

Unlike with any other bad habit I can think of, you cannot get much support in morphing your self-talk into something neutral or even beneficial. You will never be saved from it by a prince on a white steed. Every time a temptation to skip your new disciplines arises, remind yourself about the "not much" life you had because of your faulty self-talk.

Resignation equals going back to the status quo. And the status quo is an illusion. If things don't get better, they worsen. If your self-talk brings you down, it will not keep you at a constant level. It will take you to the ground level and then below.

Improving your self-talk is a task for the rest of your life. Don't dwell about this in a panic. It's like maintaining your health, a necessary element of being alive. You breathe, you drink, you move, you eat, and you watch your thoughts. That's reality. You don't get scared about the reality, you don't wail about it, you live with it.

RULE NUMBER TWO: CREATE YOUR PLAN OF ACTION

I can give you some guidelines and some of them are pretty iron-clad. But it is still your job to fit your plan into my guidelines and modify it, if it suits your needs. The only truly unbreakable rule is that whatever you attempt to do, your aim is sustainability. Remember, self-talk will never go away, and you will live with it forever. Thus, you need daily disciplines that can potentially last till your last day.

Take, for example, my journaling. I can journal ten to fifteen minutes a day, every day. I have done that for the last five years. But I couldn't have sustained one hour of journaling a day.

I wholeheartedly advise you not to bite off more than you can chew. Start with one thing. Preferably something that feels easy for you. Meditation is really easy, but plenty of people have internal bias against it. If that's you, skip it and begin with another method. Smiling is not in the first spot by accident. It's the easiest thing you can do, the easiest one to repeat many times a day and to habitualize. You should skip this method only if you already have this habit well-established.

Pick one thing at the beginning.
You may be this unicorn who can develop a few or several new habits at once. But it's unlikely. All experts and practitioners say

that trying to create more than one new habit at a time is the quickest way to burnout and failure. You cannot afford that. Your self-talk will not take a vacation to allow you to put yourself together for another attempt. Fixing your internal dialog is a full-time job. Be smart and start with one habit at a time

I've coached more than 100 people one-on one. My experience is congruent with research on this topic: it's much easier to develop a new habit if you do it daily. It's even easier if you practice it many times a day. When you skip even one day in your routine, the level of difficulty jumps drastically. I estimate that developing a daily habit is ten times easier than developing a six-day-a-week habit.

Practice every day.
Whichever method you choose, practice it every single day. Be silent yesterday, today, tomorrow, and the day after. Smile yesterday, today, tomorrow, and the day after. Keep your gratitude journal yesterday, today, tomorrow, and the day after. Take no breaks. Keep going. Developing a habit is a struggle only for the first few months. Then it becomes automatic and will serve you for decades to come.

You must be as persistent as your self-talk is. It will not go away, nor will you stop in your quest to tame the voice in your head. Your subconscious will always initiate a dialog with your conscious self. Make sure you will always have methods to deal with it.

Your new habits may be childishly easy. What is hard about smiling or keeping your mouth shut for a minute? But don't neglect essential elements of habit development.

Consciously design a trigger for your new habit.
Always track the habit in construction. The trigger is what releases your new behavior. It's important to always have the same trigger. Your habit will take less time to create and will become automatic more quickly.

I smile whenever I see a person in front of me. If someone is looking at me and our eyes meet, there is no power in the world to stop the corners of my mouth from rising up. I hammered this trigger into myself through countless repetitions. Developing this habit wasn't easy or natural for me. It took conscious effort to force a smile on my face. But the trigger was crystal clear: Someone in front of me? Someone looking at me? Then I smile.

The power of habit is such that after some time you stop thinking and automatically do. Yesterday I passed a workmate at the office, someone I had never seen before. I smiled at this guy and only realized I had when he unexpectedly smiled back.

If you use a proper trigger, a very clear one, it will create associations in your brain lighting quick. It will also solidify your new habit like concrete.

By far, the best trigger for your new habit is the endpoint of an existing habit. I journal in the morning as part of my morning routine. I do a quick and intensive series of bodyweight exercises, gulp a glass of water, weigh myself, go to my home office, open my journal, and write. I fill my gratitude diaries in the evening when I'm wrapping my day. I step away from my laptop, grab my journals, and fill them while sitting in the living room in front of the TV (my wife wraps up her days by watching TV).

I meditate on my commute to work, usually when I wait for a train on a platform. If I arrive too late to secure a suitable waiting period, I meditate on a train till the train arrives to the next station. I had trouble with meditation on weekends, when I don't commute to work. So on weekends, I changed my trigger and meditated myself to sleep, either when I caught a nap or went to bed in the evening.

My meditation trigger is not consistent, thus this is not the most solidified habit of mine. Especially over the weekends, I need an additional pinch of mindfulness to remember to do my meditation.

Keep a record of your new habit.

The other necessary component is tracking. Even if it's an activity as simple and numerous as smiling, you somehow need to sustain your awareness about this activity. Your conscious attention is like fertilizer for your habit. And tracking produces this fertilizer.

In the most basic version, all you need to do is to mark a day in your calendar if you did your discipline. You can track and mark every instance of your new behavior, or you can simply mark the day if you did it at least once.

For example, when I was overcoming my shyness, my basic discipline was to smile at strangers. Sometimes I did it twice in a day, sometimes dozens of times. But it was enough for me to smile at least once to mark this activity as done.

On the other hand, when I was practicing silence, I marked in a notepad each time I opened my mouth and uttered words.

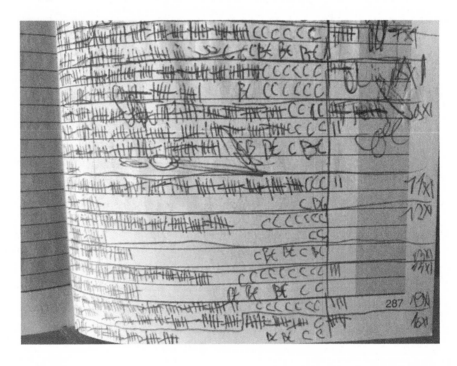

Then, at the end of the day, I counted the strokes. I also had a special category of interactions, when I couldn't let myself be quiet or drawl my words, like during business meetings. I marked them, as well, in my notepad.

Tracking the occurrences is a must, but you don't have to finish at that. I always teach that your tracking shouldn't be more complicated than the habit itself. It's counterproductive to put an ounce of effort into developing a new habit and a pound of effort into tracking it. But if you feel like it, if you see the need, you can make it more elaborate or pesky, as I did with tracking my silence (or rather breaches of silence).

I track my writing output every day. I don't simply note that I wrote. I register the start and end time of my writing sessions, where and what I wrote, in which language, and how many words I produced. I also keep track of my daily and monthly writing output, not just a record of particular sessions.

You may be so meticulous about your meditation: you can write down the times, the length, which method you used, how you felt before and after, and what the most common uninvited thoughts going through your mind were. You may be meticulous about tracking any of the six methods I provided.

Or you can be very frugal with your tracking. I don't track my journaling at all. I don't need to. The entries in my journal are the track record of themselves. I open my journal at a given day (I use simple book calendars for journaling) and I know if I journaled or not. I track my gratitude journaling in the Coach.me application by a single mark—it was done, or not. I do that because I keep three gratitude journals and opening them all just to check if I did them today seemed like an overkill.

You don't need to track your self-talk modifiers forever, but the initial period is crucial. You don't need to provide fertilizer to a grown tree as often as you provide it to a sprout. At the beginning you need to cultivate your newborn habit with attention and focus provided via tracking.

So, how long should you track your new activity? The best answer, while not very specific, is: as long as it takes to make the new discipline automatic. If you meditate, smile, or journal almost without thinking because it is what you've done today, yesterday, and for the past three months, and it is what you will do the next day, you don't really need to track your habit.

But you may. A grown tree needs some fertilizer as well. I've been writing every single day since 23rd September 2013. I've written over 1,800,000 words since I started. But I have no intention of giving up on tracking my writing sessions. Tracking an established habit provides something other than simple awareness—it provides motivation. I love to see how the overall word counter keeps increasing in my tracking sheet with each passing day. I love to say I'm a writer, and because I write and have the necessary supporting evidence to demonstrate it, it's not just empty bragging.

You may quit on tracking when you establish your habit, or you can keep it as a motivator that will help you to absorb this new habit into your core identity.

CHAPTER 10

THE POWER IS YOURS

We are human beings. We breathe all the time. We talk to ourselves all the time. It won't change soon, like the body shape of our species won't change soon.

We have two arms and two legs. We talk to ourselves. Our emotional brain (called limbic by scientists) and conscious brain communicate with each other around the clock.

And we cannot bypass this process, at least not without a miracle. Besides, it is what makes us humans in the end. There is no sense in wishing you were a tiger or an angel when you are a human. Deal with it. Live with it. Take control of it.

Not controlling your thoughts is like not controlling your arms or legs—it seriously cripples you. Imagine your life without use of your arms and hands. Imagine your life if you could not control your legs and go wherever you wanted to go.

The same rule applies to your thoughts. If they wander aimlessly all the time, or even worse, if they bombard you with vicious messages around the clock, you are disabled.

It's not the end of the world, especially if you live in a world of disabled people. Most of us suffer from a damaging internal tirade, so you probably don't even notice how limited you are by your self-talk. If everyone around you has no legs or arms, like you, it's normal, and you just try to make the most of the situation.

You cannot help, however, but notice people around you who have every limb and use them effortlessly. And there are people among us who have expanded beyond themselves because they overcame their vicious self-talk.

People cannot grow their limbs (yet), but they can change the train of their thoughts.

TAKE OVER THE STEERING WHEEL

You can change the train of your thoughts. Of course, not altogether and not right now, but that's not the point. A newborn cannot use his limbs efficiently at the beginning. It takes a strenuous trial-and-error process before a baby is able to grab a toy or walk. And you, without training your mind, will continue being unable to control what you are telling yourself.

Have you ever seen a baby that gave up on mastering his hands or quit learning how to walk? It has never happened in the history of this world.

Despite the fact that newborns are hopelessly unsuited to walking or performing complex activities with their hands (like tying their shoes), they never quit. Don't quit. It's the consistency of your actions, not the sheer size of them that brings results. Keep trying to improve your self-talk. Every positive input is priceless in the dark world of your self-talk.

Your refusal to give up will bear fruit. How much do you need to think now to take a step? How much do you need to focus to pick up a mug of tea and raise it to your lips? You barely notice it at all. Improving your internal dialog may be as automatic for you as using your legs to walk. In the end, you will be able to leverage your self-talk to your advantage in the same way you are able to run now— automatically, with just a pinch of additional effort and coordination.

Your goal is to uncripple your life for good. You won't quiet down your internal voice. You will gain an ability to communicate with it like with any other civilized person. You won't squash your self-talk, it's impossible, at least if you want to still be sane. You will change your internal voice into someone more reasonable, less emotional, and more logical.

You will gain the power to steer your mind and, in effect, to steer your life. It will take you out of the paralysis caused by constant internal criticism. You will start to make things happen in your life, things that were unimaginable, like overcoming your shyness or becoming a writer. Oops, those are examples from my life. You will start doing different things that were impossible for you. Ask a bedridden person what they would do if they could move? The possibilities are endless.

You are unique. You have amazing talents waiting to be put into use. They wait only because you stop yourself from utilizing them. You can do simple things and amazing things. You can lose weight. You can support others in their quest for excellence. You can get rid of your addictions. You can develop new skills. You can spend more time with your kids. You can earn more. You can love like Christ. You can change the world.

Whatever you are after, your chances will significantly increase when your self-talk starts to support you. Who knows? Maybe you will master it to a degree that it will support you in the pursuit of your aspirations.

CHANGE YOUR INTERPRETATION

Controlling all your self-thoughts is as impossibly hard as controlling an arm's movement 24/7. It's theoretically possible, but you'd do nothing else. It defeats the purpose. If you focus 24/7 on controlling your arm's movements, you will not have an ounce of attention to spare for the rest of your body... and the rest of your life. The methods I've taught you are habitual. They aim to habitually deflect your damaging self-talk or morph it on a subconscious level.

You don't need to consciously focus on your arms' movements to take advantage of them. When you walk, your arms are moving on autopilot, helping keep your balance. You've been practicing moving your arms while walking since you were a toddler. You don't need to focus on them unless you are drunk or other special circumstances occur. The same applies to your self-talk. Once you learn to control it, your habits will work to your advantage in the background of your mind.

You cannot simply strangle your negative self-talk. And you don't need to. My default thinking option is still "I'm a worthless failure." I had been thinking this thought for decades, and it's not simple to eradicate it. But nowadays, I respond differently to it. I learned this new way and consciously worked to change it. My habitual response is now: "Right! But worthless or not, I'll do it anyway!" Ninety-nine percent of your self-talk is aimed for passivity. The words in your head intend to keep you in check, so your fears prevail and you do nothing.

I choose not to be passive. My firm conviction is that if I do nothing, nothing can change for better and plenty can change for worse. Thus, whenever my old "worthless" narration emerges, I acknowledge I heard it and steadily do my own thing.

And the whole point of the negative narration is missed. I act instead of being passive. My self-talk no longer cripples me. And the more I do, the less basis there is for my negative self-talk. It was easy to believe my subconscious stories when they were never confronted with reality. Now, when I do more, I become "less of a loser." There is no supporting evidence for my vicious internal voice. Hence, the negativity of my self-talk decreases with time. I don't need to be constantly on my toes, because my self-talk simply shuts up more often than not. And sometimes, which is a true miracle, it's even reluctantly supportive: "Heck, you succeeded again, maybe you are not as full of sh*t as I've thought."

I'm far from being a master of my internal dialog. I'm not yet at the level of Tony Robbins who seemingly can talk himself into all kinds of successes. But I significantly dropped the level of emotional turmoil in my life caused by what I tell myself. My self-talk didn't change enormously, I still talk to myself like a drunken felon all too often. But it doesn't hurt me as much as in the past.

And most importantly, it doesn't stop me right in my tracks. I act. I'm above the whispers in my head. *I* steer the direction of my life, not the random thoughts that are bouncing inside my skull.

I want the same for you. Take action. Start building new habits. Smile, meditate, shut up, keep a gratitude journal, journal every day, work on your vocabulary regularly. Free yourself from the shackles of self-bullying. Start doing what you desire to do, not just things that are so easy that you cannot fail.

By adopting those habits in the process of grappling with your self-talk, you will build other handy qualities helpful in life in general. Your focus will increase. You will get to know yourself better. Your health will improve!

Just begin. Take action. Keep going. That's the only success formula you'll ever need.

Godspeed!

LINKS

Research about smiling
https://www.psychologicalscience.org/news/releases/smiling-facilitates-stress-recovery.html

Coach.me about meditation
http://blog.coach.me/getting-started-with-meditation/

How to keep a "perfect" gratitude journal
https://medium.com/personal-growth/how-a-one-minute-action-changed-my-life-completely-68c1a699e587

Jim Rohn about poor self-talk
https://www.success.com/rohn-how-to-stop-listening-to-the-negative-voice-in-your-head/

Jim Rohn about vocabulary
http://www.accessnewage.com/beststeps/Beststep.cfm?bs=842

Vocabulary and learning
http://www.ascd.org/publications/books/113040/Chapters/What-Does-the-Research-Say-About-Vocabulary%C2%A2.aspx

Ohio State University study about vocabulary
https://www.sciencedirect.com/science/article/pii/S0740547216300290

The same study in layman words
https://www.thecut.com/2016/12/when-excons-change-their-vocabulary-they-stay-out-of-jail.html

'Hidden' benefits of silence
https://psychcentral.com/blog/the-hidden-benefits-of-silence/
https://www.ncbi.nlm.nih.gov/pmc/articles/PMC1860846/
https://www.researchgate.net/publication/259110014_Is_silence
_golden_Effects_of_auditory_stimuli_and_their_absence_on_adul
t_hippocampal_neurogenesis

CONNECT WITH MICHAL

Thanks for reading all the way to the end. If you made it this far, you must have liked it! I really appreciate having people all over the world take interest in the thoughts, ideas, research, and words that I share in my books. I appreciate it so much that I invite you to visit www.expandbeyondyourself.com, where you can register to receive all of my future releases absolutely free.

Read a manifesto on my blog and if it clicks with you, there is a sign-up form at the bottom of the page, so we can stay connected. Once again, that's

www.expandbeyondyourself.com

MORE BOOKS BY MICHAL STAWICKI

A Personal Mission Statement: Your Road Map to Happiness

Trickle Down Mindset: The Missing Element In Your Personal Success

The Art of Persistence: Stop Quitting, Ignore Shiny Objects and Climb Your Way to Success

99 Perseverance Success Stories: Encouragement for Success in Every Walk of Life (with Jeannie Ingraham)

Get Rich Quotes for Every Day of the Year from The Science of Getting Rich

Six Simple Steps to Success series:

Free vol. 1: Simplify Your Pursuit of Success

Vol. 2: Know Yourself Like Your Success Depends on It

Vol. 3: Bulletproof Health and Fitness

Vol. 4: Making Business Connections that Count

Vol. 5: Directed By Purpose

How to Change Your Life in 10 Minutes a Day series:

Free: The Fitness Expert Next Door: How to Set and Reach Realistic Fitness Goals in 10 Minutes a Day

Learn to Read with Great Speed! Only 10 minutes a day!

Release Your Kid's Dormant Genius In Just 10 Minutes a Day: Parenting Your Smart Underachiever With Consistency and Love

Master Your Time In 10 Minutes a Day: Time Management Tips for Anyone Struggling With Work-Life Balance

From Shy to Hi: Tame Social Anxiety, Meet New People, and Build Self-Confidence

A SMALL FAVOR

I want to ask a favor of you. If you have found value in this book, please take a moment and share your opinion with the world. Just let me know what you learned and how it affected you in a positive way. Your reviews help me to positively change the lives of others. Thank you!